No part of this publication may be reproduced or transmitted in any form or by any means, electronic or mechanical, including photocopy, recording or any animation storage and retrieval system, without prior permission from the authors.

Author: Barbora Klima Bratova   Illustrator: Lucy Pirogova

First edition: 2023

## Dedication:

To my children, who were medically kidnapped for six months by Family and Children's Services of the Waterloo Region, one of the many corrupt "child protection" businesses in Ontario.

To P. for making it through.

To Dr. K. Nolan and Dr. B. Baird, CAAPs at McMaster hospital. There is a special place in hell for you two.

To Dr. D. Callen and Dr. A. Howard who fell into their trap instead of making their own, independent, opinions first.

To S. McLean, the assistant Crown attorney, for her decision to prevent my children from seeing or communicating with their Dad for years while waiting for trial.

To P. Kiatipis, the long-term director of the Child Welfare Secretariat in Ontario, for turning a blind eye to the dysfunction and ignoring those who call it out.

To Mariana, Elena and Sandu for their fast response, and Veronika, Michal and both grandmas for the long-term help. We wouldn't have been able to go through it without you all.

To Monika S. for her kind guidance in the time of grief.

To Matinka, bandičky, Jiřulka and Dagmar for their shoulders to cry on.

To bababi for believing in miracles.

To all the therapists for believing in E. and helping him overcome obstacles.

To my dear fellow fighters from the Stop Medical Kidnapping group.

To all the parents who have been, are, or will be fighting this fight. You've got this. Please speak about your experience publicly.

To all the good doctors and parent advocates out there who decide to go against the system.

Special thanks to Dr. Marvin Miller, Dr. Michael Holick, Dr. Jane Turner, Dr. Joseph Scheller, Dr. Charles Hyman and to Mr. Phillip Millar from Millar's Law and his team for making everything well again.

# Rickie's Rickets Journey

Medical kidnapping series:
Vitamin D deficiency/ infantile rickets

Author: **Barbora Klima Bratova**   Illustrator: **Lucy Pirogova**

When Ricardo the Owl was born

- a couple of weeks earlier than was expected -

he was just a tiny little owlet.

"Rickie, dear," his Mom and Dad whispered to him,

"welcome to the world."

"We couldn't wait to finally meet you."

"We love you so so so so much."

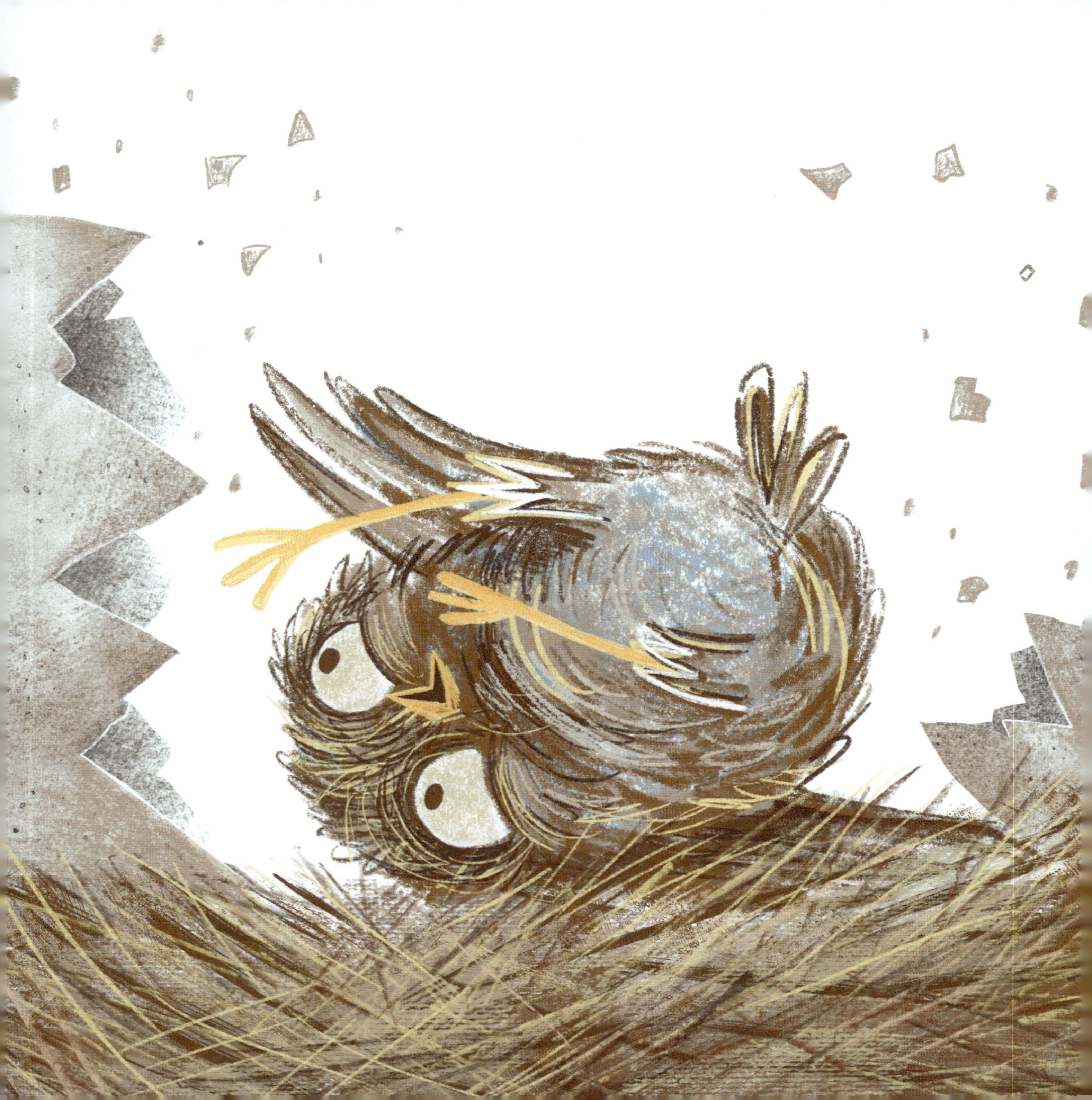

Rickie grew...

...and grew...

...and grew.

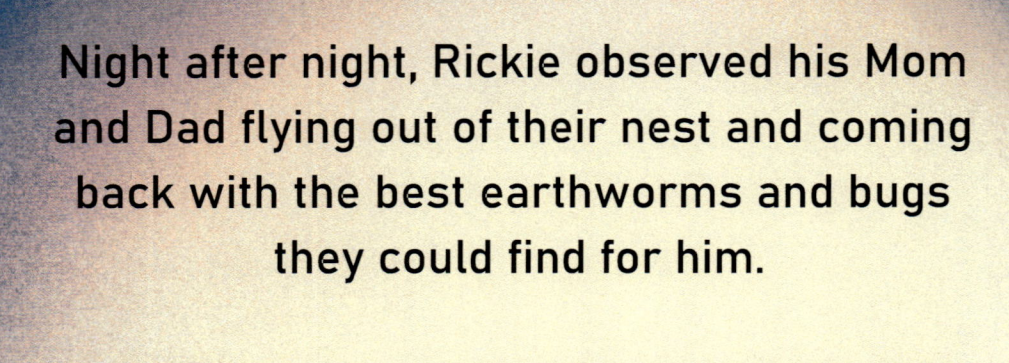

Night after night, Rickie observed his Mom and Dad flying out of their nest and coming back with the best earthworms and bugs they could find for him.

"Mom, Dad, can I fly yet? Can I? Can I?"

"Soon, very soon," Rickie's Mom and Dad answered. First, your feathers and wings need to get big and strong. Don't forget to do your flapping exercises."

There was no need to remind Rickie. Flying was on his mind all the time.

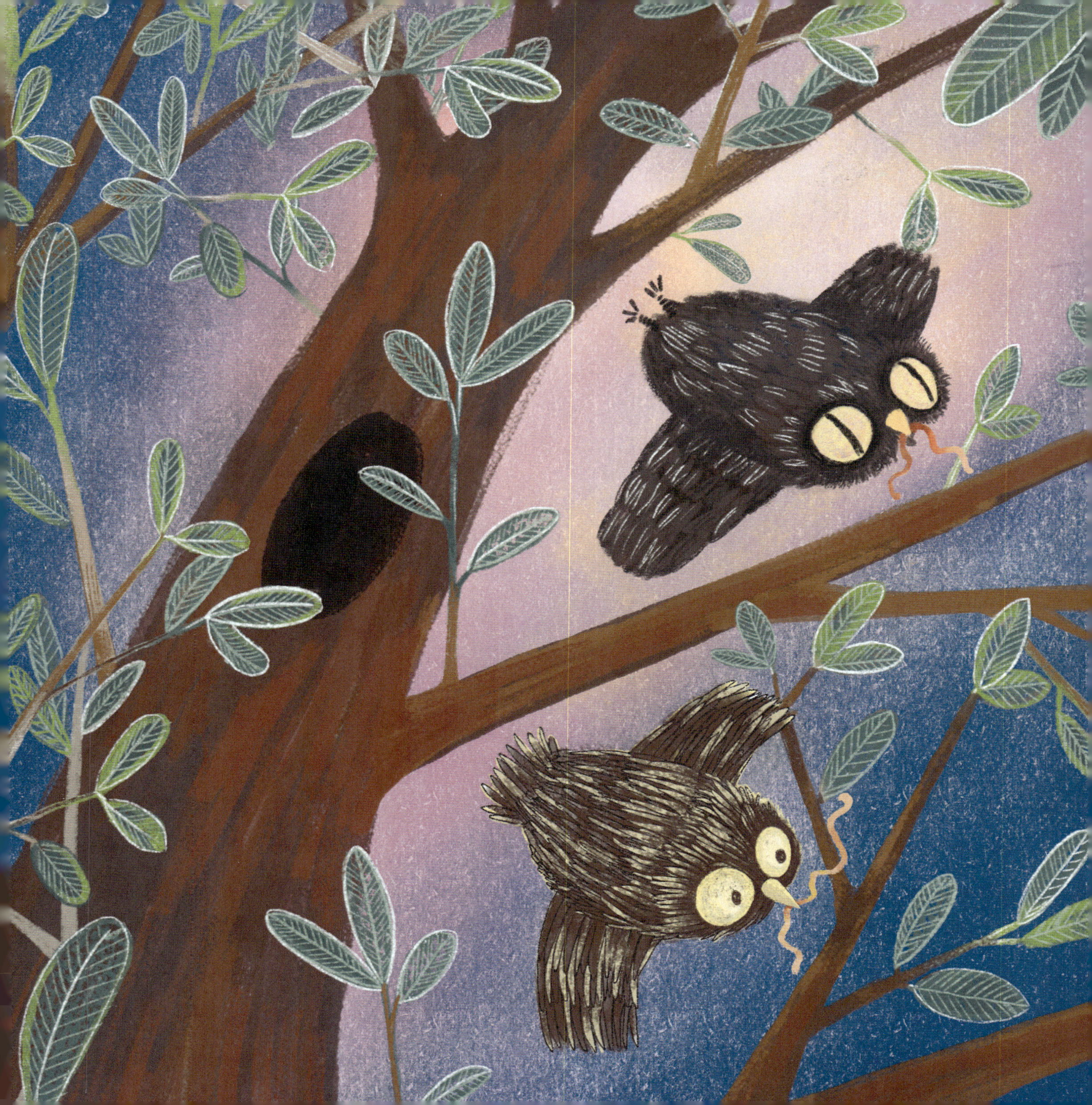

Rickie had passed all his Well Owlet Checkups at the forest doctor's office with flying colors. He didn't enjoy the examinations too much, but it was always over fast enough. "I have no concerns," the forest doctor noted every time. "Rickie is growing big and strong."

At Rickie's 10-week checkup, the forest doctor examined his feathers and wing span. "Rickie's feathers are nice and healthy," the forest doctor told Mom and Dad. "His wings are strong."

He turned to Rickie: "Good news, buddy. You are ready to fly and hunt yourself. Your Mom and Dad can start teaching you any day now."

Rickie couldn't be any happier. "Hooray! That's going to be the absolute best day ever!"

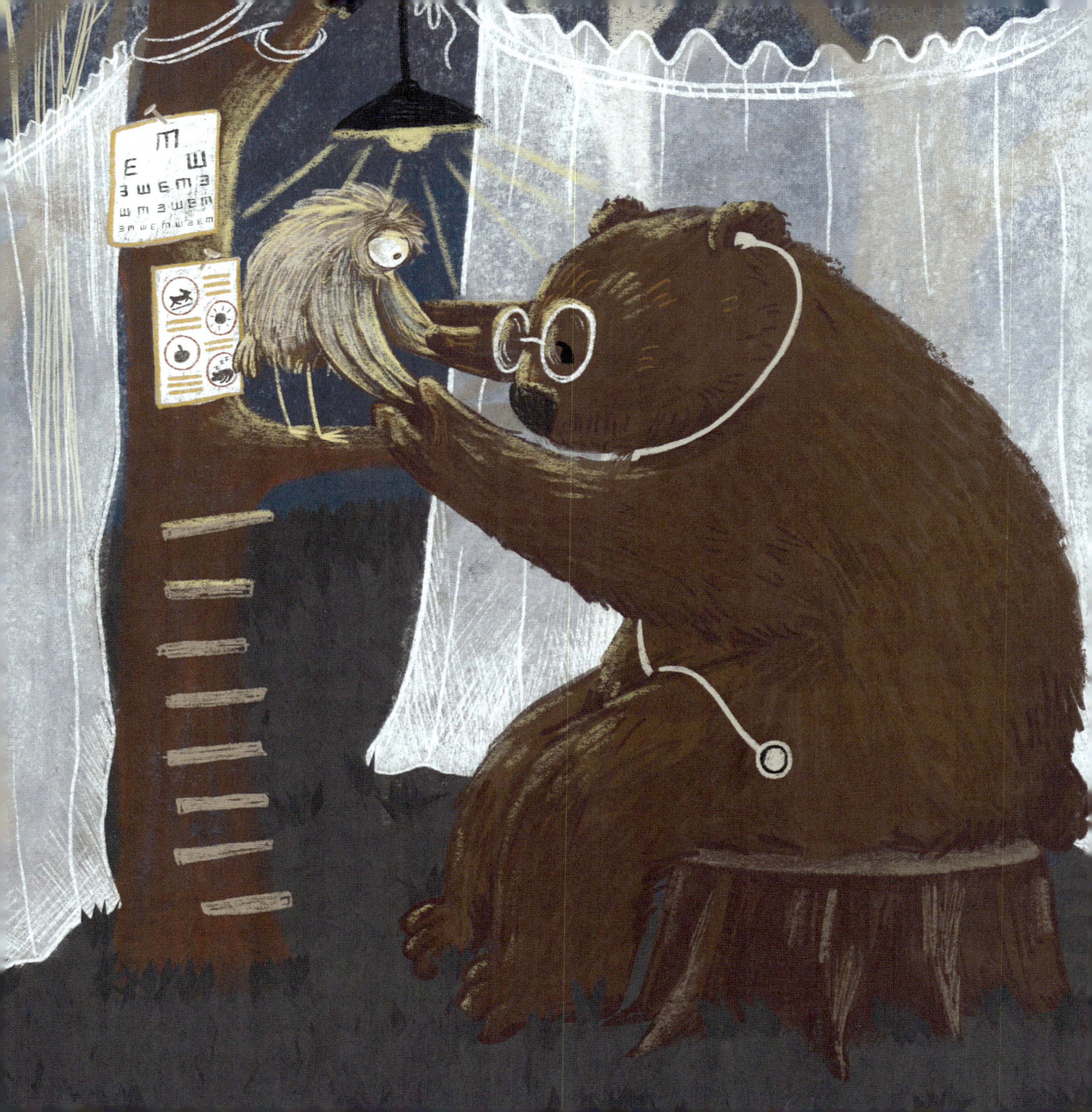

The big day has finally come. Rickie was ready to learn to fly.

He hopped around, excited to try.

"You've got this," his Dad encouraged him.

Rickie jumped into the air, trying to flap his wings fast enough to fly.

"Ouch, ouch!" Rickie cried out.

"What is it, Rickie?" asked his Dad.

"I'm not sure I can fly today after all. My right wing hurts."

Back home, Dad told Mom all about Rickie's first try at flying. "Rickie did so well getting into the air. But then his right wing started to hurt when he flapped really fast."

"Well, that's not good," Mom thought.

"Let's go see the forest doctor to make sure Rickie's wing is ok," Mom and Dad agreed.

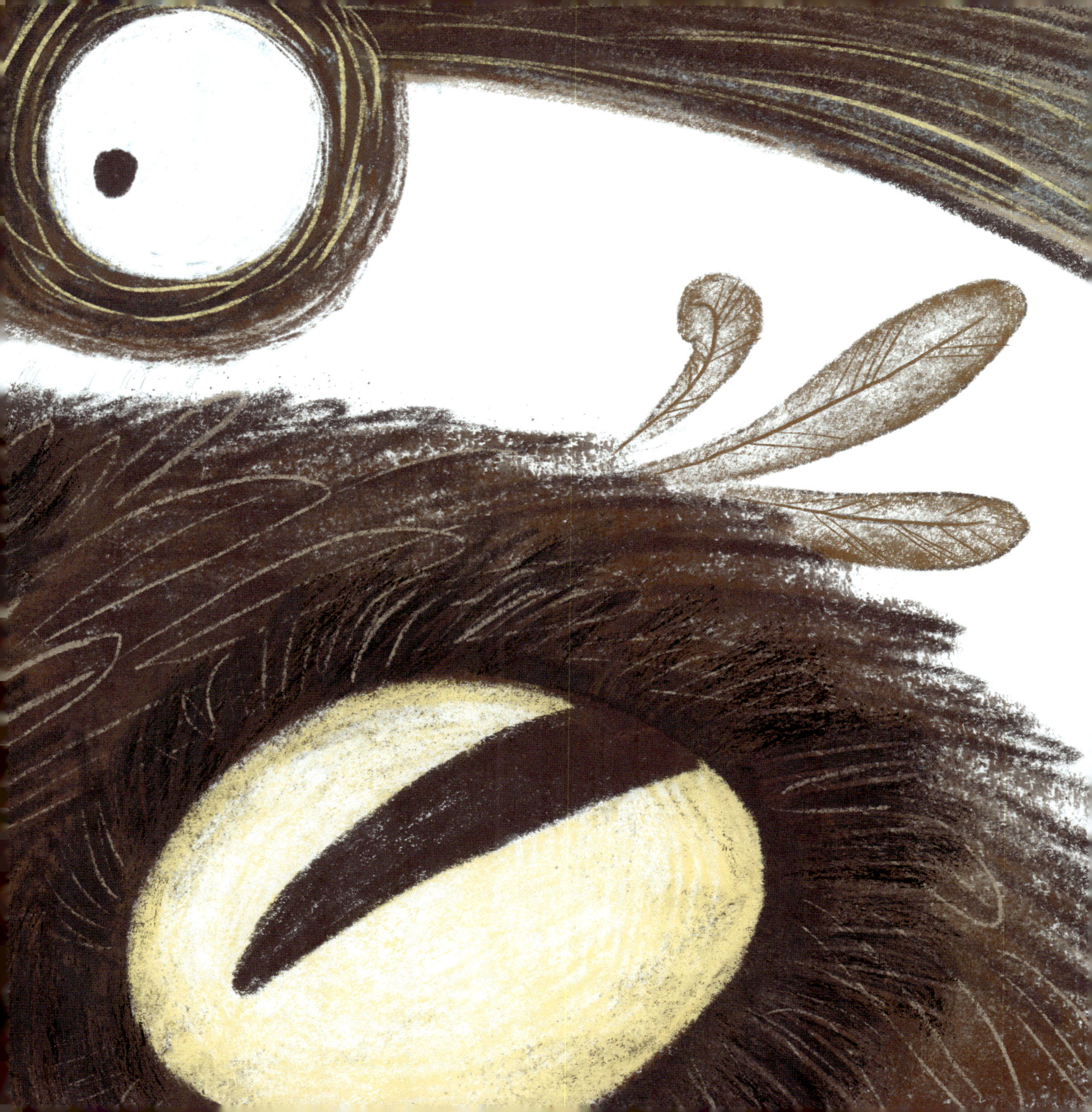

"Oh dear, the forest doctor's office is closed today. We'll have to go to the city hospital instead," Rickie's Mom whispered, concerned.

Mom and Dad carefully wrapped Rickie into an Owlet carrier and flew to the city to get help.

The city hospital X-rayed Rickie's wing. When Dr. Stoneheart, one of the city hospital pediatricians, brought back the results, she looked very worried.

"Well, Rickie's wing seems to have a fracture," she said. "Do you have any explanation for that?" she asked Mom and Dad.

"What's a *CRACK-ture*, Dad?" Rickie wanted to know.

"A fracture means a broken bone, Rickie," his Dad shook his head in disbelief.

"Are you sure, Doctor?" Rickie's Mom asked, confused. "Rickie has had no accidents, no bruises or swelling. He just tried flying for the first time earlier today."

"He had passed all his Well Owlet Checkups," added Rickie's Dad, shrugging his shoulders.

"No explanation? Well then, it must have been *you* who hurt Rickie's wing," Dr. Stoneheart stated firmly.

Rickie's Dad was stunned, "Excuse me? No, we didn't hurt Rickie! Absolutely not!"

"There must be something wrong with his bones. We would like a second opinion, please!"

Dr. Stoneheart didn't say a word and left the room, closing the door behind her.

When the door reopened, in came a stern, scary stranger. "I'm Patricia Murky, an Owlet Protection Worker. I need to talk to Rickie. Alone."

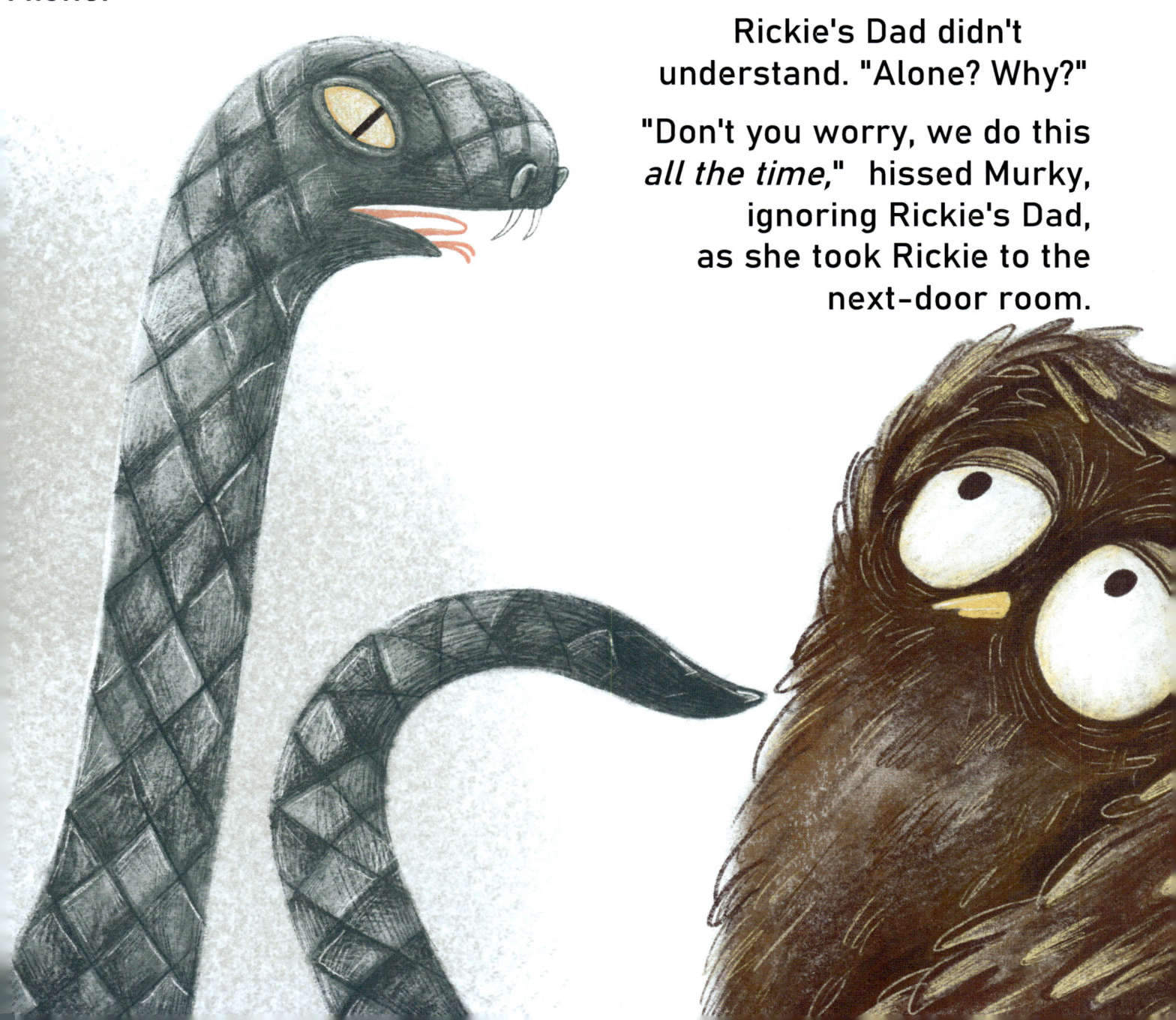

Rickie's Dad didn't understand. "Alone? Why?"

"Don't you worry, we do this *all the time*," hissed Murky, ignoring Rickie's Dad, as she took Rickie to the next-door room.

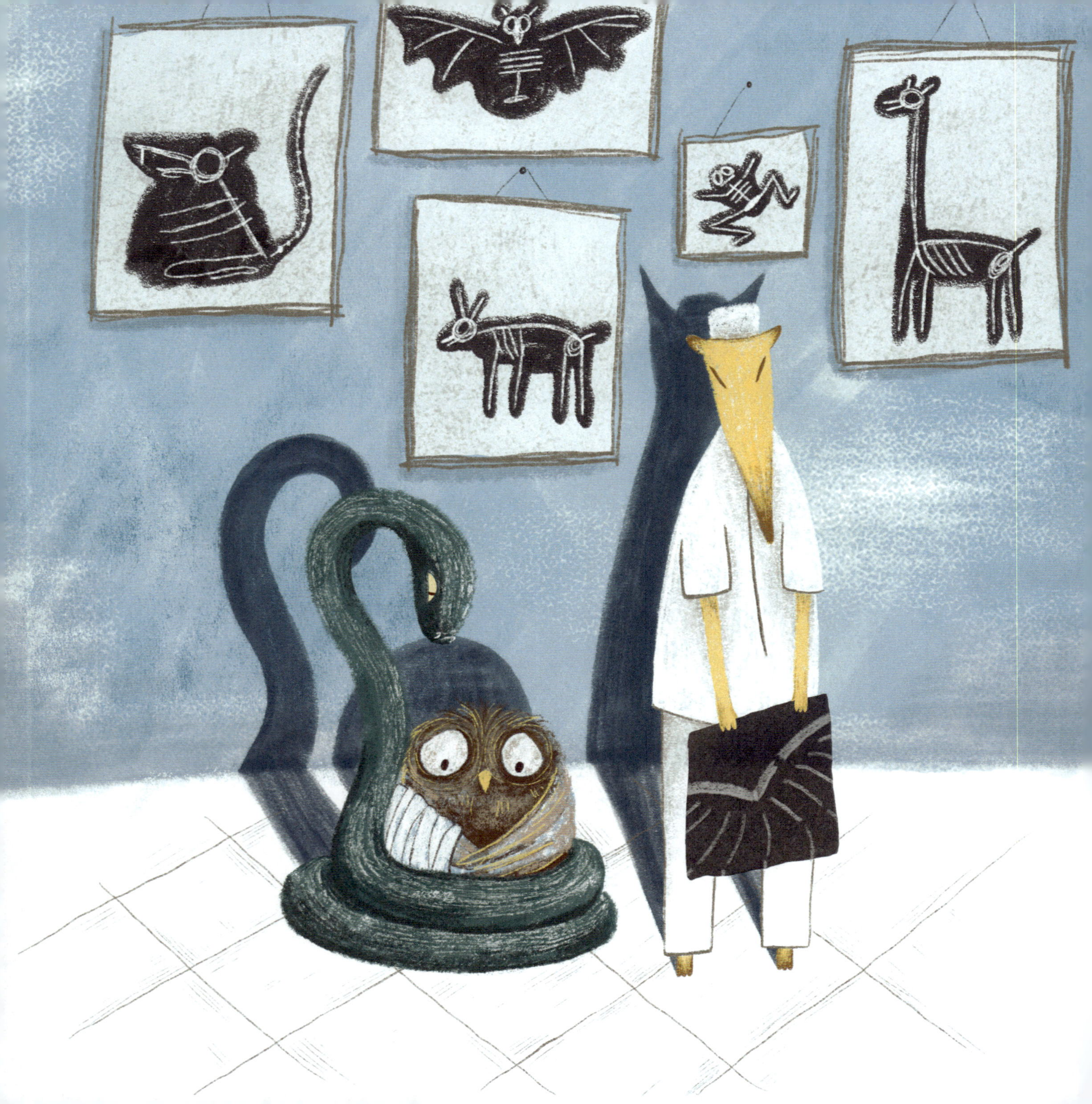

A short time later, Murky and Rickie returned. "I have finished my investigation. Rickie is at risk of harm with you. He told me you'd *squeeze* him all the time," Murky stated.

Rickie was shocked. "No! No!! I meant Mom and Dad had *hugged* me me all the time. I never said they squeezed me to hurt me."

"I will have to apprehend you, little one," added Murky.

"*UPPER*-hand me? What is that? Rickie was confused.

"I will be taking you away with me," hissed Murky.

"Mom and Dad never hurt me!" Rickie yelled. "They never ever hurt me," he repeated, scared stiff as Murky dragged him away.

Murky ignored Rickie. "Don't you worry, little one. We'll put you into a *very* nice foster home."

Murky and Dr. Stoneheart turned to Mom and Dad: "Leave now!"

"No! Please! We need to see another doctor. Please!" repeated Dad.

"We cannot leave Rickie here, all alone," cried Mom. "He's just a little owl. His wing hurts. He needs us. We never hurt him!"

"Oh sure. I hear this *all* the time," laughed Murky.

"Rickie! We will be back! We love you!"

"Don't be so dramatic," added Murky as she pushed Mom and Dad out the door.

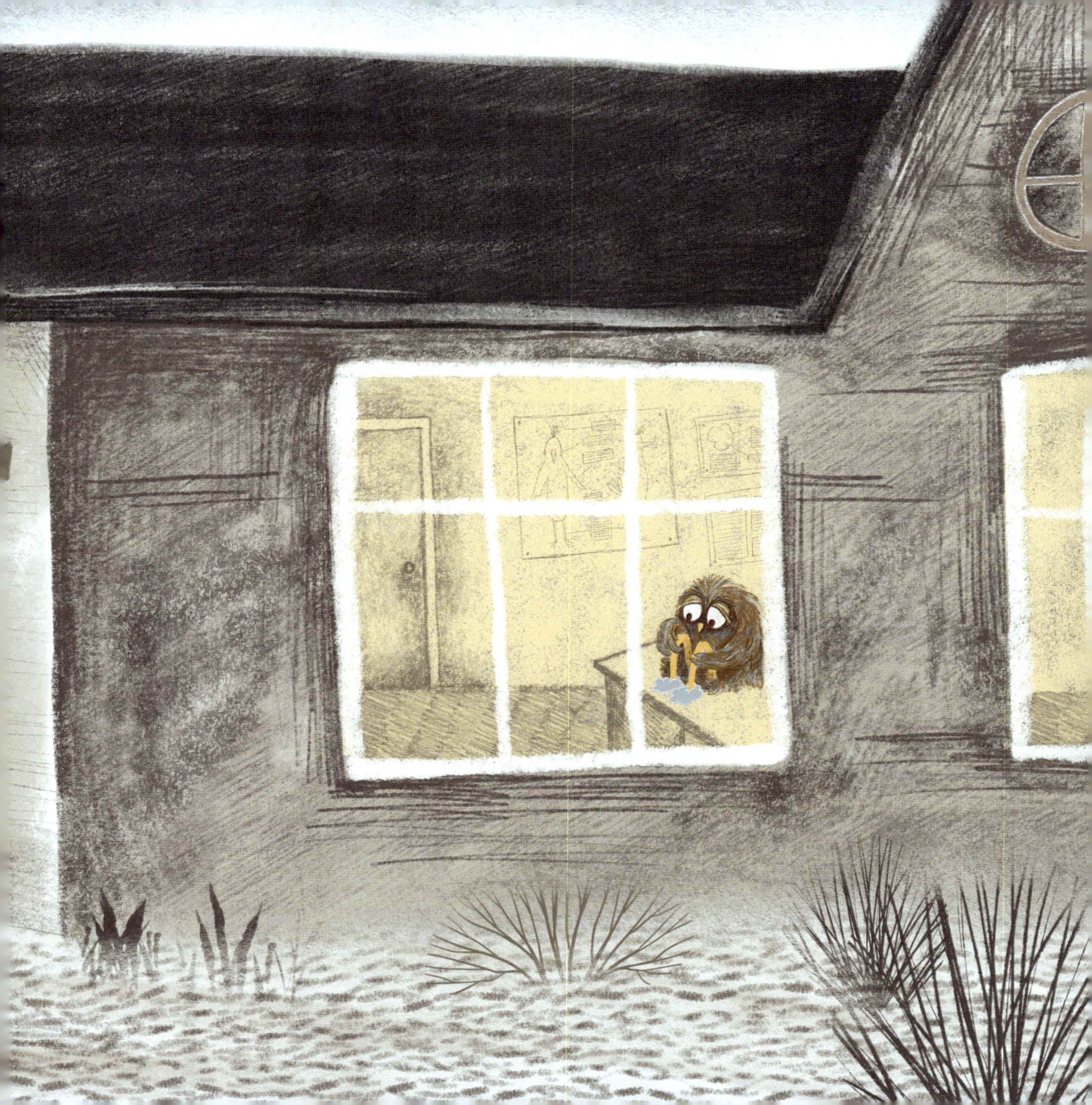

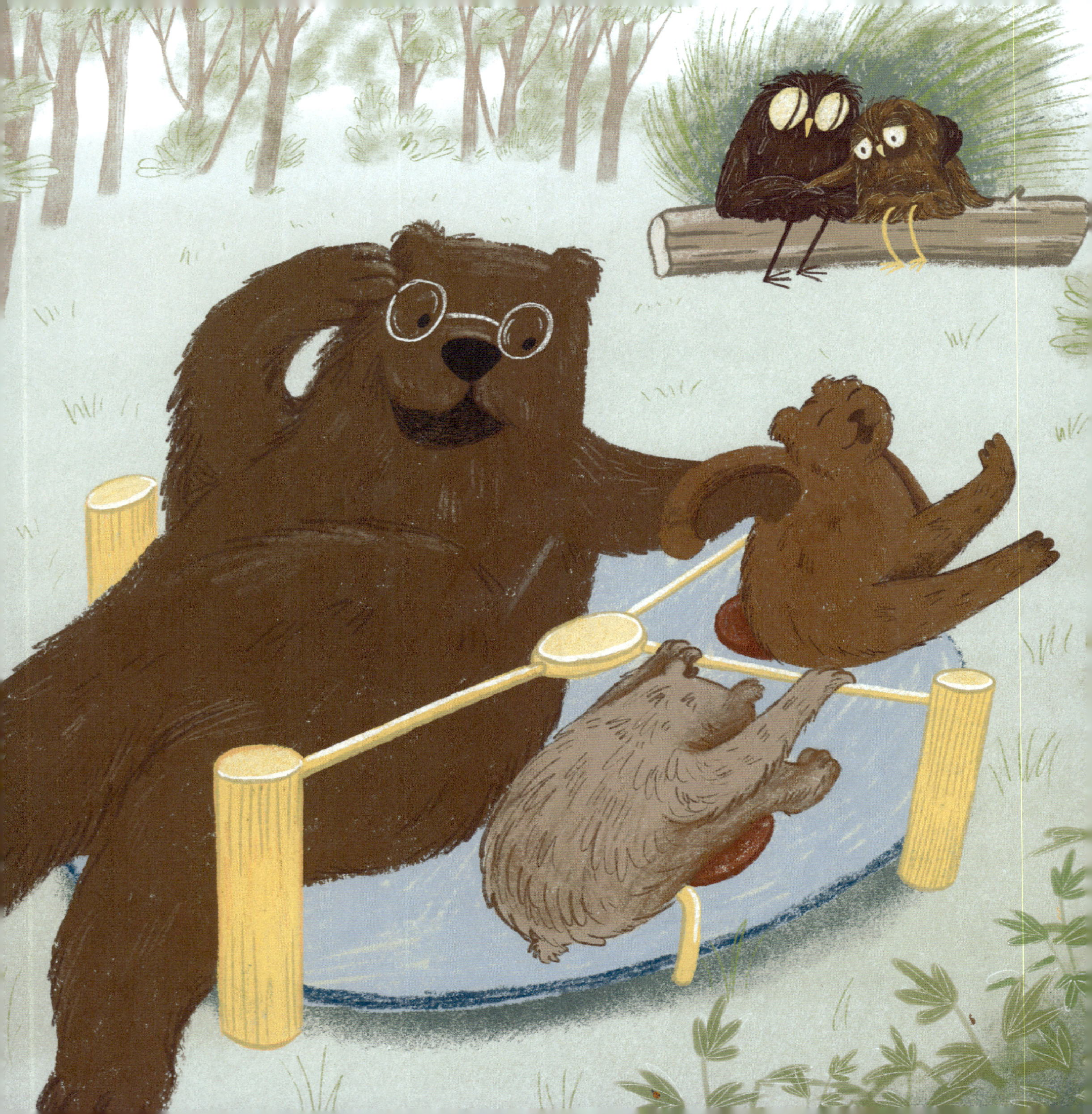

Mom and Dad missed Rickie very much. They could only see him twice a week at the Owl Protection Centre where Murky observed them.

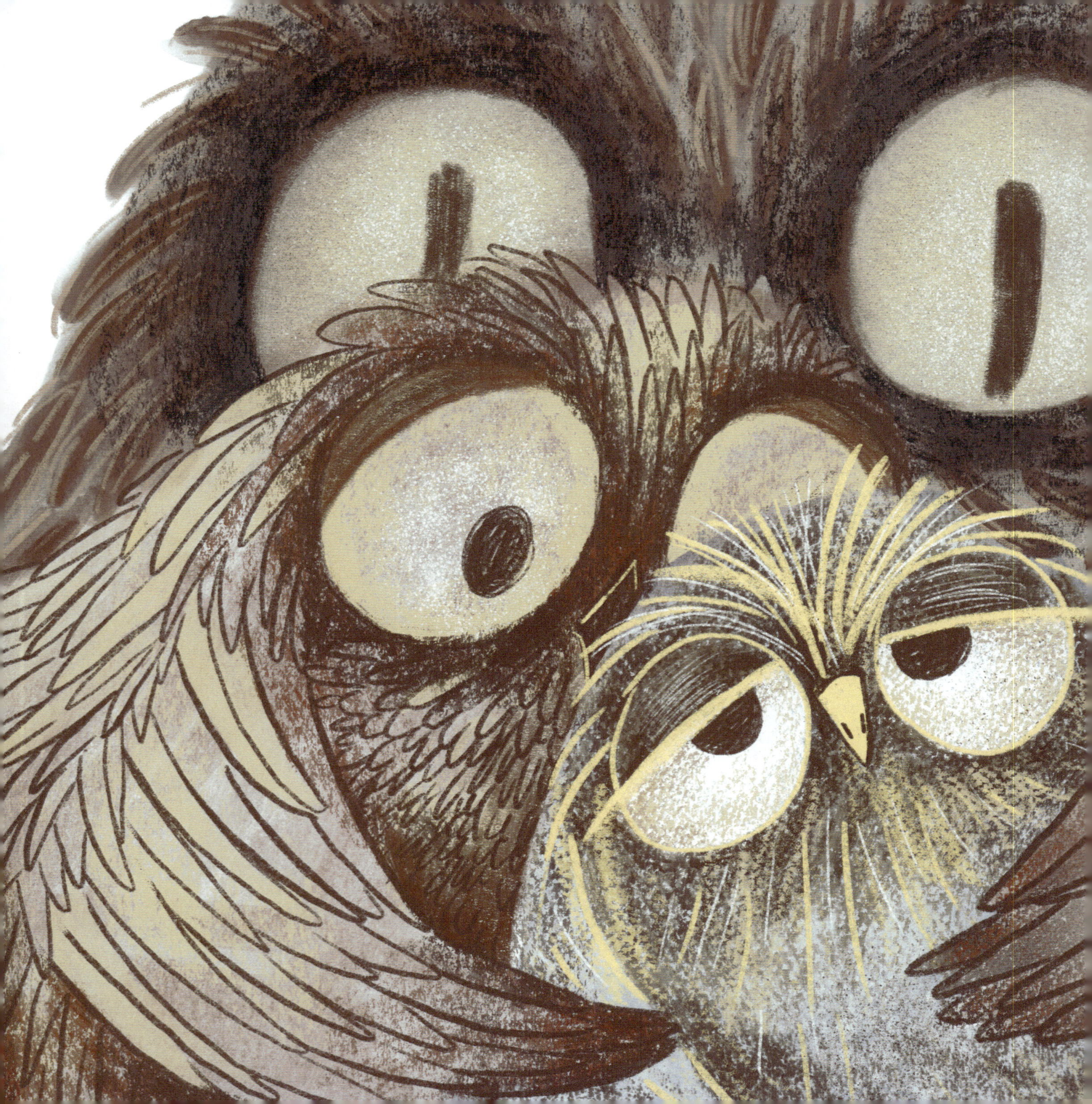

At every visit, now that his wing had fully healed, Mom and Dad gave Rickie a huge hug and held him for a long time. "Mom, Dad, can I come back home? Can I? I don't like the foster home. I miss you."

"We miss you too, Rickie. We love you so, so much. We are doing everything we can to find out what happened to your wing and bring you back home," said Mom.

"We have a special helper called *a lawyer.* Lawyers know a lot about the rules that adults need to follow. He will help us get you back home," added Rickie's Dad.

Mom and Dad squeezed Rickie tight again as their visit slowly came to an end. "We will see you next week. We love you."

At one of the next visits at the Owl Protection Centre, Mom told Rickie, "Good news! Our lawyer has found a bone doctor, called Dr. Wiseman, who helped us understand what was wrong with your wing."

"You see, we want our bones to be as strong as the thickest branches in our home tree. Yours were more like dry twigs, because your body didn't have enough vitamin D. That's a super vitamin that helps make our bones nice and strong," explained Dad.

"Yes," continued Mom, "your bones were so weak that they got tiny cracks when you first fell out of your egg, when we carried you and when you were practicing flapping."

"Oh no, that means I'll never be able to fly," thought Rickie to himself as he listened to his Mom and Dad.

"Don't worry," Mom saw his sad face, "with extra vitamin D, your bones are getting stronger every day and you will be able to fly without any problems," she added, as if she read his mind.

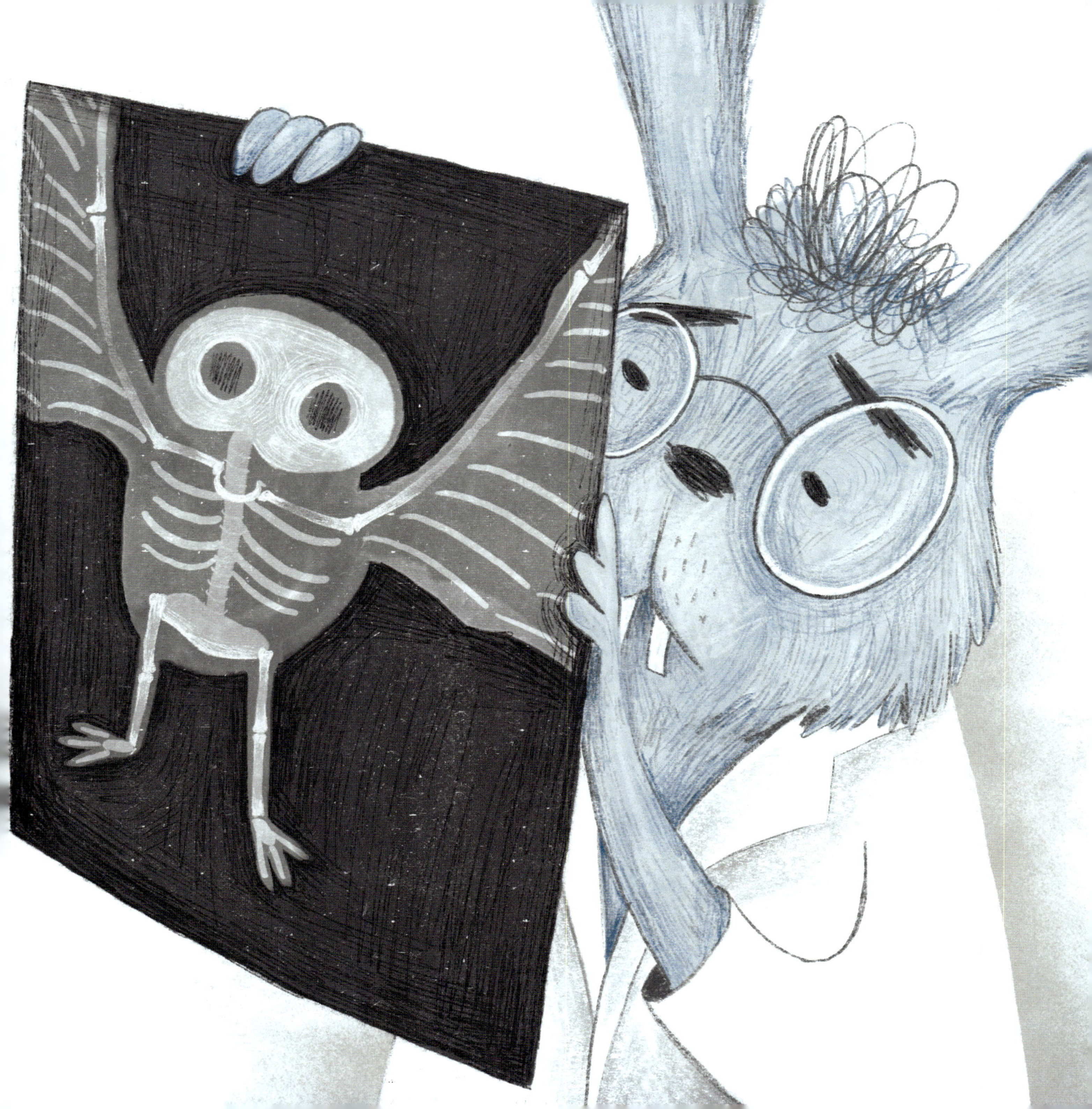

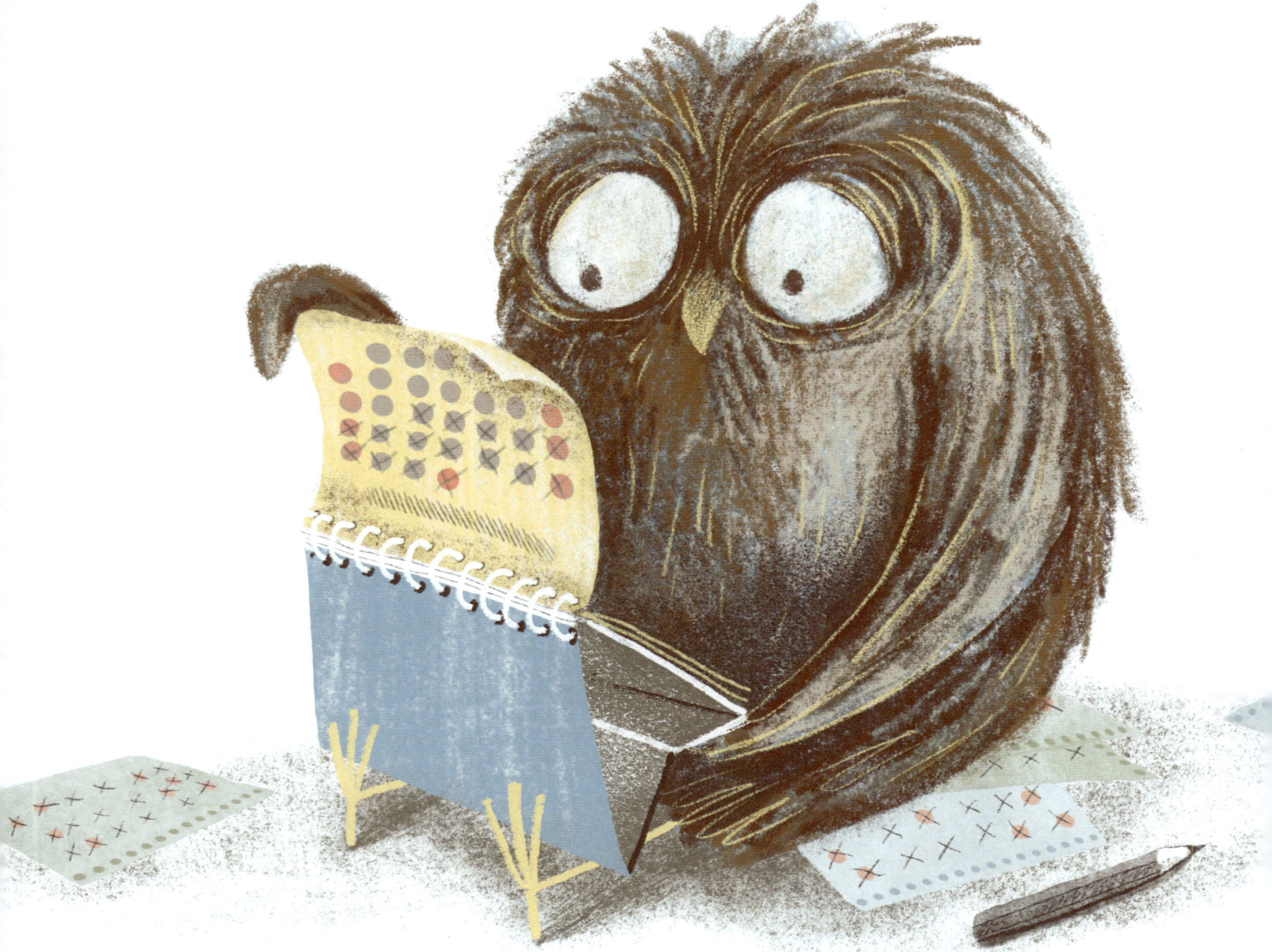

Rickie knew that his Mom and Dad and their special helper, the lawyer, had to go to a place called court. There, a special referee called a judge, would listen and decide what happens next.

The Owl family couldn't wait for the court date to come. Rickie was counting sleeps. Birthdays, holidays and Christmases had passed before the big day arrived.

Dr. Stoneheart and Murky told the Judge they thought Rickie's parents had hurt him. "There is no other explanation for his wing fracture, judge," Dr. Stoneheart said, with a sly smile.

"Yes, there is," replied Dr. Wiseman. "Rickie was sick; he had infantile rickets. His bones show all the typical signs and he had very low vitamin D levels."

The forest doctor nodded along in agreement.

The judge carefully listened to both sides and then waved his trunk at Murky and Dr. Stoneheart.

"Ricardo the Owl shall be returned home right this minute. His Mom and Dad did not hurt him. He had infantile rickets."

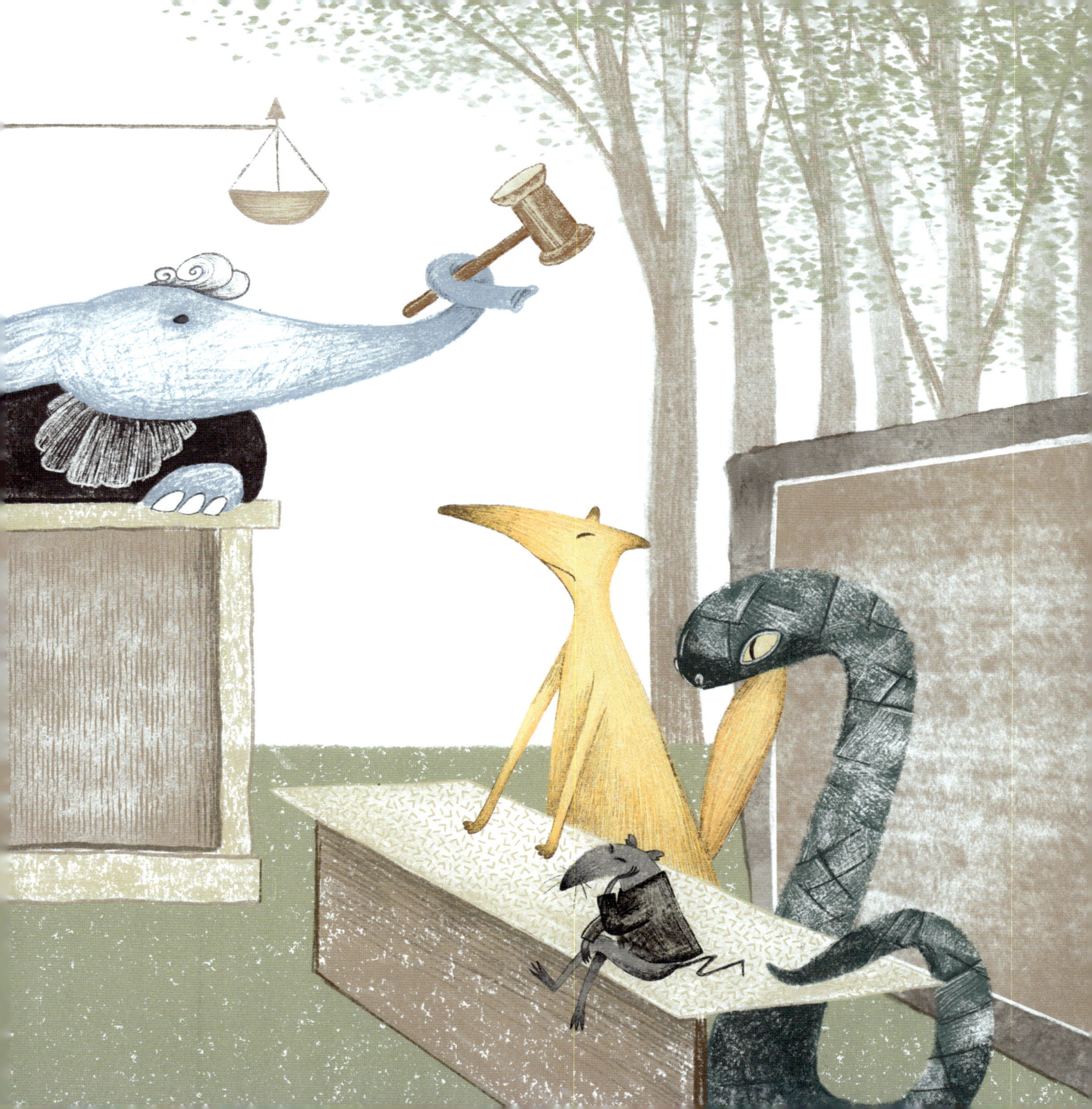

The Owl family couldn't be any happier, back together at last.
"It's been a long journey. It's time to heal now and tell our story. We hope that what we've been through won't happen to anyone else."

## Questions for children:

1) Hi! Thanks for reading our book! How did Rickie's story make you feel?
2) Were there any parts that surprised or confused you?
3) How do you think Rickie felt?
4) Can you think of a time in your life when you very much felt you were right about something and found out you were wrong? If so, what did you do when you found out?
5) Can you think of a time in your life when one of your friends or an adult made a mistake but meant well?
6) Doctors know so much and help people get better. Can they ever be wrong? If so, what should they do when they find out?

## Questions for parents who have been through medical kidnapping:

1) How did Rickie's story resonate with your own experience?
2) How did your family cope during the process?
3) Did you get justice in the end? What steps did you take to get justice?
4) Has your family healed? What steps did you take to heal?
5) What advice would you give other parents who find themselves in a similar situation?

## Questions for parents who have NOT been through medical kidnapping:

1) Have you ever met any family impacted by medical kidnapping?
2) If so, did you have a hard time believing them because of what the authorities (doctors, child welfare, or the police) said?
3) Do you think medical kidnapping can ever happen to you? Why? Why not?
4) Do you agree that parents should be treated as innocent until proven guilty?
5) Would you be willing to support law changes that advocate for second medical opinions before apprehensions?

## Information for parents and caregivers:

### medicalkidnappingontario.ca
### stopmedicalkidnapping.ca
For resources, personal stories and media coverage related to medical kidnapping cases in Ontario, you can visit medicalkidnappingontario.ca. Similarly, stopmedicalkidnapping.ca, provides information on a Canada-wide scale (coming in 2024).

### CTV W5 episode "Dubious Diagnosis"
Families based in Canada and USA tell their stories of medical kidnappings of their sick, misdiagnosed children; the author's family was included in this project.

### Fractured Families - Facebook group
Support for those with children with unexplained/misdiagnosed fractures.

### "Powerful as God" - documentary
The film reveals a child welfare system plagued by systemic and bureaucratic abuse that urgently requires public attention. Financed by tax dollars and wielding extraordinary power, the Children's Aid Society is deconstructed to reveal a broken system where employees have been heard to describe their influence over children and families to be as powerful as God.

### "Protecting Your Child from the Child Protection System" by B.A. Maloney, J.D.
Essential information on how to protect your child, especially if your child is sick or medically complex. Written by a lawyer with over 20 years of experience in child protection cases.

### "The Syndrome" - documentary
How false abuse accusations by child abuse pediatricians tear families apart.

### "Take Care of Maya" - documentary
Maya Kowalski, a ten-year-old girl diagnosed with complex regional pain syndrome, was wrongly labeled a victim of abuse by the child abuse pediatrician Dr. Sally Smith. The misdiagnosis lead to Maya's unjust hospitalization, mistreatment by the hospital staff, and forceful separation from her parents, especially her mom, Beata Kowalski, the alleged abuser. Tragically, Beata took her own life. The Kowalski family sued Johns Hopkins hospital, and in 2023, they won their case.

## Author: Barbora Klima Bratova

Founder of Stop Medical Kidnapping.
medicalkidnappingontario.ca
stopmedicalkidnappping.ca

"My life turned around by 180 degrees after my son's strokes and infantile rickets were misdiagnosed as child abuse in 2017. Since then, my life mission has become educating the public on the danger of medical kidnappings by CAS/CPS and child abuse pediatricians, advocating for accountability of CAS and for legal changes to prevent medical kidnappings."

1 day before birth

67 days before medical kidnapping

photo: M.Lungu

## Illustrator: Lucy Pirogova

"I've always looked for myself in creativity. Since childhood I loved to draw, but I didn't know where and how I could apply it. Illustration is probably the best thing I've been able to find for myself. I love finding a visual language for completely different stories: sometimes they are fun fairy tales, sometimes cautionary tales, and sometimes serious life stories.

I hope that this book will evoke empathy for everyone in the reader. And I really believe that such situations will remain only in books, and only good things will happen in our lives."

Manufactured by Amazon.ca
Bolton, ON